D0534487

DOGS

DISCARDED

LAKE OSWEGO JR. HIGH SCHOOL
2500 SW COUNTRY CLUB RD
LAKE OSWEGO, OR 97034
503-534-2335

Scientific Consultant:
Dr. Karen Overall
Behavior Clinic, School of Veterinary Medicine
University of Pennsylvania

Picture Credits

American Kennel Club—Page 10
Bill Anderson—Page 12
Kent & Donna Dannen—Pages 7, 9, 14, 15, 16-17, 18, 19, 20, 21, 24-25, 25, 26, 27, 29
Ron Kimball—Cover; Endpages; Pages 6, 7, 8, 11, 13, 14, 14-15, 15, 16, 19, 20, 20-21, 21, 22, 27
Zig Leszczynski—Pages 18, 19
Jim & Marlene Lyons—Page 8
Reynolds Photography—Page 17
Lynn M. Stone—Pages 7, 13
UPI/Corbis-Bettman—Page 17
Kim Heacox/DRK Photo—Pages 6, 22
Lisa Husar/DRK Photo—Pages 10-11
Gary R. Zahm/DRK Photo—Page 13
Jeff Christensen/Gamma Liason—Page 15
Languna Photo/Gamma Liason—Pages 11, 18-19
McKierman/Gamma Liason—Page 25
Dale Spartas/Gamma Liason—Page 12
Zimbardo Xavier/Gamma Liason—Page 24
The Granger Collection—Page 7
International Stock—Pages 17, 27
Tom Carroll Photography/International Stock—Page 28
James Davis/International Stock—Pages 26-27
Manuel Denner/International Stock—Pages 6-7
Bob Firth/International Stock Photo—Page 16
Michele & Tom Grimm/International Stock—Page 23
John Guider Photography/International Stock—Page 12
Ray Solowinski/International Stock—Page 28
Mary Bloom/L&I—Pages 10-11
Yoram Kahana/Shooting Star—Page 25
John D. Cunningham/Visuals Unlimited—Page 10
Patrick J. Endres/Visuals Unlimited—Pages 12-13
Bill Kamin/Visuals Unlimited—Page 11
Steve McCutcheon/Visuals Unlimited—Page 9
Tucson Bud Nielson/Visuals Unlimited—Page 25
Wm. S. Ormerod, Jr./Visuals Unlimited—Pages 17, 29
N. Pecnik/Visuals Unlimited—Page 23
Kjell B. Sandved/Visuals Unlimited—Page 9
John Sohlden/Visuals Unlimited—Page 22
Ned Therrien/Visuals Unlimited—Page 23
Miriam Zook/Visuals Unlimited—Page 20
Henry H. Holdsworth/The Wildlife Collection—Page 26
Gary Schultz/The Wildlife Collection—Page 23

Copyright © 1997
Kidsbooks, Inc.
3535 West Peterson Ave.
Chicago, IL 60659

All rights reserved including the right of
reproduction in whole or in part in any form.

Manufactured in the United States of America

EYES ON NATURE™

DOGS

Written by
Philip Koslow

kidsbooks®
Incorporated

MAN'S BEST FRIEND

Throughout human history, dogs have been given the freedom to live in our homes, sleep on our beds, and walk with us side by side. They fetch the balls we throw, lick our faces, and wag their tail in joy. The dog has always been man's best friend.

FAMILY MATTERS

Wolves, coyotes, jackals, and foxes are all part of the same family as the dog. In the wild, these *canids* live and hunt in small groups and show powerful loyalty to their leader.

HEROIC HOUNDS

When they became domestic animals, dogs transferred their inborn sense of loyalty to the humans they lived with. There are countless true stories of heroic dogs dragging people from burning buildings, saving them from drowning, and defending them from attacks—even at the cost of their own life.

Balto carried medicine in Alaska during the winter of 1925.

GETTING TOGETHER

Dogs and humans have lived side by side for more than 12,000 years. Most likely, this relationship began when wild canids joined human hunters in pursuing game. Realizing that these clever animals could be highly useful, humans started taming them.

TOP TO BOTTOM

Dogs come in an incredible range of sizes. The massive St. Bernard (right) can tip the scales at 200 pounds or more, while a tiny Pomeranian (top) might weigh as little as three pounds.

HOLY HOUNDS ▼

In ancient Egypt, dogs were treated as sacred beings. The pharaohs' own pups wore jeweled collars, ate the finest food, and had their own servants to wait on them. When the pharaohs died, their favorite dogs were often buried with them in magnificent tombs.

The Egyptian god Anubis, with the head of a jackal, was said to guide souls of the dead to their judgment.

In Japan, the akita was thought to have great spiritual powers.

CUSTOM-BUILT CANINES

Humans began breeding dogs to emphasize special traits and talents. There are now more than 400 separate breeds of dogs, not to mention the mongrel, or mutt, which combines characteristics of many breeds. And there are lots of dogs. In the United States alone, there are more than 50 million!

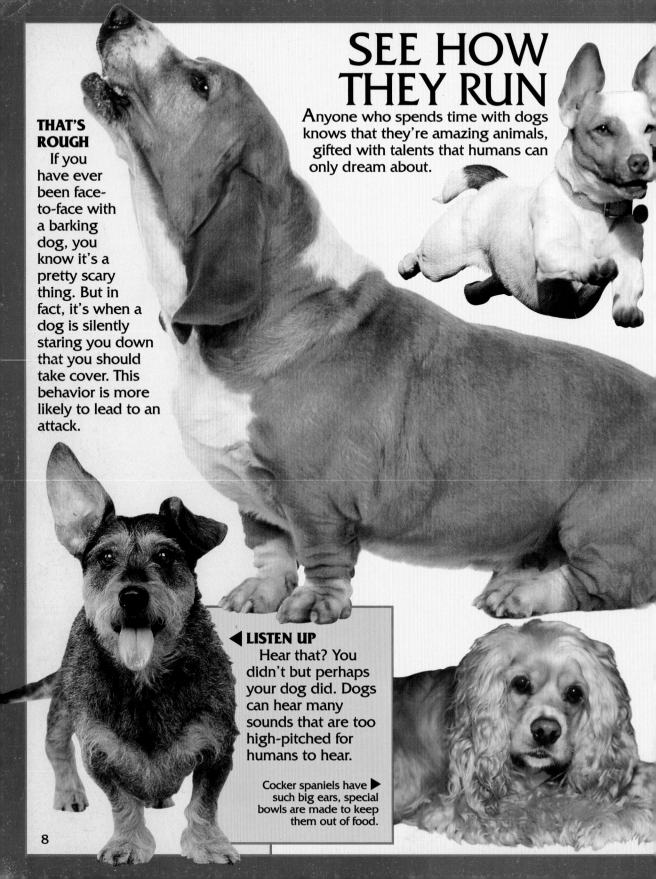

SEE HOW THEY RUN

Anyone who spends time with dogs knows that they're amazing animals, gifted with talents that humans can only dream about.

THAT'S ROUGH

If you have ever been face-to-face with a barking dog, you know it's a pretty scary thing. But in fact, it's when a dog is silently staring you down that you should take cover. This behavior is more likely to lead to an attack.

◀ LISTEN UP

Hear that? You didn't but perhaps your dog did. Dogs can hear many sounds that are too high-pitched for humans to hear.

Cocker spaniels have ▶ such big ears, special bowls are made to keep them out of food.

...lds on the bloodhound's head help to protect ...e eyes from sharp grass as the nose sniffs a ...ent on the ground.

ALL-TERRAIN FEET ▼
Padded paws are not always full-proof protection against rocks or sharp objects. That's no problem for the fleet saluki. Salukis grow thick mats of hair between their toes, enabling them to run on any kind of ground.

SMILE!
Dogs start out with a set of 28 teeth, which begin to appear after six weeks. At six or seven months, a set of 42 adult teeth will come in. Dogs use their teeth mostly for tearing and crushing—they usually gulp food down instead of chewing it.

...NIFF, SNIFF
...A dog's sense of smell is nearly ...million times better than ours! ...e secret lies mainly in the ...ape and size of the interior ...a dog's nose, which ...ntains a tremendous ...mber of nerve endings ...nd odor-sensing cells.

OVERHEATED ▼
When we get over-heated, we sweat all over our body to cool off. But when a dog becomes too hot, it opens its mouth widely, lets its tongue flop over the side, and pants. The mois-ture which builds on the tongue is very similar to sweat.

WINTER WARDROBE
Dogs have a built in year-round wardrobe that grows according to the light of day. In summer, a dog's coat grows slowly. As the days get shorter in the fall, a dog's coat grows quickly. In the spring, winter coats begin to shed in preparation for the warm weather.

◄ Shar-pei means sharkskin or sandpaper in Chinese—a good description for the dog's coat.

HERDING DOGS

For more than 9,000 years dogs have held jobs as sheep and cattle herders. The key to training a herder is to manage the dog's natural desire to hunt—good herders stalk their charges and may even nip at them, but they never attack.

CANINE WAITER ▼

Originally bred for herding sheep, the Shetland sheepdog is extraordinarily clever and can be taught the names of specific items in order to fetch them on command.

SEEING THE LIGHT ▲

Old English sheepdogs peer at the world through a curtain of hair. It doesn't cramp their style, though. Dogs rely on smell and hearing much more than sight. And hair is good protection for the eyes when scurrying sheep kick up clouds of dust.

◀ MIX AND MATCH

What do you get when you mix a collie with a dalmatian and a wild dingo? The perfect herder. The Australian cattle dog was bred for this purpose in mind. And since the 1800s, this dog has been known for its stamina and faithfulness.

BELGIAN CHOCOLATE ▲

If you're a dark dog and want to herd sheep, you'll be great at your job. Sheep respond best to darker colors. The Belgian sheepdog makes a very good herder for this reason. It's also been a good soldier. During World War I, Belgian sheepdogs served on the battlefield by carrying messages and medical supplies and even pulling machine guns.

TOP DOG ▲

The border collie is so intelligent it can carry out dozens of different commands. This, and their ability to work sixteen-hour days, makes the border collie one of the finest herding dogs in the world.

PRINCE OF ▶ WALES

One of the world's oldest breeds, the Welsh corgi has roamed the hills of Great Britain for the last 3,000 years since arriving with Celtic invaders from central Europe. Though its legs are short, the corgi's long back makes it a fast runner.

INSTANT ID ▲

One of the most unusual-looking dogs in the canine kingdom, the puli (POO-lee) has a soft, woolly undercoat and a long, coarse outercoat. When both coats grow out, they form a ropelike mass. The puli has been a swift and agile herder for more than 1,000 years.

11

IN THE HUNT

Many centuries ago, when humans lived in small bands as hunter-gatherers, dogs skilled in hunting were a huge asset. Many hunting breeds are still prized for their special skills and unique temperaments.

▼ These beagles get ready to set out for the hunt.

HOT DOG

Though the dachshund makes a playful house pet, it was first bred as a hunter. Its long body was designed for trips down badger holes. At one time dachshunds weighed as much as 40 pounds, and they were known to tackle fierce wild boars.

GET THE ▶ POINT

When pointers sniff out game birds, they stand absolutely still with their body and head aimed right at the prey. The classic pointer was bred in England, Spain, and eastern Europe during the 17th century.

A German short hair pointer on the job.

◀ THE GRAY GHOST

Nicknamed the gray ghost for its coloring, the silky-smooth weimaraner is a fairly new breed, dating back only to the 1800s. It combines the keen nose of the bloodhound with the pointer's talent for flushing game.

SWIMMING LABS
It's no wonder Labrador retrievers are great swimmers. Originally, they were trained to retrieve fishing nets through icy waters on the coast of Newfoundland.

SETTER
Setters were originally trained to crouch down in front of game birds, so that hunters could trap the birds with nets. Later, they learned to point. The Irish setter has a thick coat which allows it to follow a trail through shrubs and thorns.

SLEEPYHEAD
With their floppy ears and big, sad eyes, basset hounds may look like they're always ready for a nap. In fact, these dogs are energetic hunters that will follow the scent of a pheasant or hare through the thickest undergrowth.

WORKING DOGS

Herding and hunting have kept dogs busy through the ages, but that's far from all they do for us. Their loyalty, courage, and special talents make them a natural for jobs that help to improve people's lives.

NEW WORLD DOG

Powerful swimming machines, Newfoundlands are legendary rescue workers. With their water-shedding coat and webbed feet, these dogs can swim through anything. They've saved countless lives by hauling exhausted swimmers and shipwrecked sailors out of the water.

▼ A FRIEND IN NEED

In the rugged Swiss Alps, St. Bernards have been helping injured skiers and climbers for more than 300 years. They lie down next to unconscious victims and lick their face, providing warmth and stimulation until help arrives. Barking and whining will call attention to the injured person, and if that doesn't work, search parties will organize to look for the missing dog.

FIRE! ▼

Also known as firehouse dogs, dalmatians have been hanging out with firefighters since the days of horse-drawn water pumpers. Long before that, dalmatians were coaching dogs, running tirelessly alongside carriages as guides and guardians.

▼ K-9

The German shepherd's strength and intelligence have made it the first choice of police departments and the military. Specially trained shepherds can track down wanted criminals, sniff out illegal drugs, and uncover hidden explosives.

HELPING HAND

One of America's most popular purebreds, Labrador retrievers make wonderful companions for people with physical disabilities. Specially trained from the time they are puppies, they fetch fallen objects, open doors, turn light switches on and off, and bring food from cabinets and refrigerators.

This seeing-eye dog provides guidance for his blind companion.

SNOWDOGS

In the Rocky Mountains, ski patrols use golden retrievers to locate skiers caught in sudden avalanches. Brought to the site of an avalanche by sled or helicopter, the rescue dogs can detect a human scent even when the victim is covered by several feet of fresh snow.

TERRIBLE TERRIERS

Hungry rodents have been plaguing farmers for count-less centuries by invading their barns and eating valuable grain. Farmers fought back by breeding terriers, small dogs with powerful jaws who could slip into narrow spaces and ferret out the invaders.

▲ The Yorkshire terrier may look innocent enough, yet this little rascal makes a brave guard dog and shows no fear of the largest canines.

ISLAND HOPPER

The cairn terrier originated on the rugged Isle of Skye. The dog got its name because it was first used to flush small animals out of cairns, the small piles of stones that the Scots use as memorials and boundary markers.

▲ CANINE COURAGE

Terriers are famous for never backing down, and many experts feel that the long-legged airedale is, for its size, the world's most coura-geous dog. Like other terriers, airedales can be snooty with strangers and other dogs, but they are fiercely devoted to the family they live with.

AMERICAN GENTLEMAN ▶

Originally the Boston terrier was bred for dog fighting. At that time these miniature dogs were called bull terriers. When the "sport" was outlawed, the bull terrier was recognized as a pure breed under the condition that the offending name be changed.

▼ PRESIDENTIAL PAL

Fala, history's most famous Scottish terrier, was the faithful sidekick of President Franklin D. Roosevelt (1882-1945). The lively little Scottie went everywhere with the president, and his life-size bronze statue now graces the Roosevelt Memorial in Washington, DC.

▼ BIG BULLY

Mixing the bulldog with a terrier produces one dog with a bad rap. Defenders of pit bulls say that these dogs are gentle unless people train them to be aggressive. Pit bulls, nonetheless, have been labeled as dangerous animals.

▲ TOUGH AS NAILS

The Bedlington terrier may look like a little lamb, but don't be fooled. It was bred by nail-makers in northern England who prided themselves on having the toughest dogs around. The first true Bedlington, known as Piper, was still hunting badgers at the ripe old age of 14.

17

BEWARE OF DOG

Dogs have been guarding the homes of their masters for a long, long time. A wall decoration uncovered in the ruins of Pompeii, an ancient Italian city, shows a fierce-looking dog with his teeth bared—beneath this scary image are the Latin words CAVE CANEM (Beware the Dog).

◄ OLD GUARD

Few guards have been on the job as long as the great Pyrenees, which first appeared in Europe nearly 4,000 years ago. In addition to protecting livestock, the great Pyrenees was used by French nobles to guard their castles—the dogs actually occupied guard posts alongside soldiers.

WAR AND PEACE ▼

Bulldogs were originally designed as fighting dogs. Over the centuries, the aggressive qualities have been bred out of them, but their courage, tenacity, and devotion are still there.

COMRADE IN ARMS ▲

In ancient Britain, mastiffs fought side by side with their masters against Julius Caesar's Roman warriors. Centuries later, when the English knight Sir Peers Legh was wounded at the Battle of Agincourt, his loyal mastiff defended him for hours until help arrived.

LEARNING YOUNG ▶

The imposing kuvasz gets its name from [T]urkish word meaning "armed guard of [th]e nobility." In Hungary, shepherds [us]ed the kuvasz as a nighttime [gu]ardian of the flocks. Placed among [sh]eep while they are puppies, the [do]gs develop a fiercely protective [at]titude toward their woolly com[pa]nions.

PULLING THEIR WEIGHT ▼

The ancestors of the rottweiler entered Germany long ago with conquering Roman soldiers and stuck around to become cattle guardians. They were also used to drive the herds to cattle markets and to pull people in small two-wheel carriages.

◀ ALL MUSCLE

The doberman pinscher was bred in Germany by crossing German shepherds with other breeds such as rottweilers and terriers. Because of their trim build, dobermans may look more delicate than some other guard dogs, but their smooth coats hide tightly packed layers of muscle.

[KI]NG OF DOGS ▶

No guardian can scare off intrud[e]rs faster than the regal great dane, [w]hich was developed in Germany [m]ore than 400 years ago as a [h]unter of savage wild boars. Today, [e]ven the smallest great danes stand [n]early three feet tall at the shoul[d]er—incredibly enough, those [e]arly boar hunters were [b]igger!

19

TOY STORY

At the small end of the scale are the toy dogs, bred originally as house (or castle) pets for kings, queens, and nobles. The idea was to produce dogs that could easily be carried from place to place and cradled on laps.

▼ Because of the golden colors in its coat, the llasa apso is referred to as the lion dog.

The pomeranian, ▶ whose average size is five pounds, acts like a big dog, even when faced with a huge rotweiller.

LITTLE LION ▶

The silky-soft shih tzu was a favorite of Chinese emperors for centuries. Shih tzu means "lion" in Chinese, but these dogs, whose weight barely reaches double figures, are sweet-tempered and docile.

LIFESAVER ▼

Another gift of the Orient, pugs were originally pets of Buddhist monks in Tibet. After being imported to Europe, the pug became the favorite dog of England's King William II, who believed that a pug had saved his life on the battlefield by sniffing out the presence of concealed enemy forces.

◀ SOUL MATE

The Chihuahua (chee-WAH-wah), which rarely weighs more than six pounds, can be traced back to the Aztecs of ancient Mexico. The Aztecs buried Chihuahuas with the dead, believing that the tiny dogs ha the power to safely guide human souls through the underworld.

20

LOYAL TO THE END ▶

English toy spaniels were favorite pets of English royalty during the 1500s and 1600s. When Mary, Queen of Scots was beheaded in 1587, her beloved toy spaniel refused to leave her side and accompanied her to the scaffold.

▼TAKE-OUT ORDER

Like the large and medium-size members of their breed, toy poodles come in a variety of colors, including black, white, blue, gray, beige, and apricot. Poodles are among the smartest of dogs, and some have been bred so small that they could fit in the sleeve of a shirt.

BUTTERFLY DOG

From its elegant ears, which resemble butter-fly wings, the papillon gets its name. At one time, these dogs were so popular in France that noblewomen would not pose for portraits unless there was a papillon in the picture.

MUSH

In the frigid region near the Arctic Circle, sled dogs are more than workers and companions—they can mean the difference between life and death. How tough are these dogs? They can sleep outdoors in a blizzard, wake up coated with ice, and be ready to run all day!

NATIVE ▶ AMERICAN

The Mahlemut Indians of Alaska developed their own sled dog, now known as the Alaskan malemute. Slightly larger than huskies, malemutes are sled-racing prizewinners.

SUPREME TEST

Every March, the Iditarod (I-dit-a-rod) Trail Sled Dog Race takes place. The course is a grueling 1,159 miles through barren Alaskan wilderness. The record for the trip is 9 days, 2 hours, 43 minutes. Throughout the race, veterinarians keep tabs on the health of the dogs—the sled drivers are on their own.

◀ BLAZING TRAILS

The brilliant white samoyed, another champion sledder, was the choice of explorers trying to find the North and South Poles in the early 1900s. A team of top expedition dogs can travel 25 miles a day over frozen tundra while pulling more than 1,300 pounds of supplies!

BREAKFAST OF CHAMPIONS

To reach peak condition, Iditarod dogs train four days a week between August and April. Their diet is monitored to make sure they get the right mix of fats, proteins, minerals, and vitamins. Amazingly, these highly trained athletes actually eat less than the average house dog.

OUT OF SIBERIA

Dogsleds were first used in Siberia, Russia, about 4,000 years ago. Somewhere in the distant past, people bred the ideal sled dogs, which are now known as Siberian huskies. To this day, they are regarded as the best for hauling light loads over long distances.

KEEPING IT SIMPLE

Sled drivers use a few clear commands to control their dogs—"gee" (turn right), "haw" (turn left), "come gee" and "come haw" (half turns), "line out" (straighten up before moving), and "mush" or "let's go" to get under way.

Before snowmobiles, Siberian huskies were able to pull sleds over long distances.

These sled dogs are taking a break.

LEADER OF THE PACK

In every sled team, the strongest dog gets to be the leader or "wheel dog." When challenged by another team member, the wheel dog will respond with a menacing growl; the challenger, if he knows what's good for him, will roll on his back and kick his legs in the air as a sign of submission.

SHOW TIME

In addition to all the work they do, dogs also strut their stuff in the show ring, at the racetrack, and even in the movies. Each year in the United States alone, more than 10,000 competitions are held to demonstrate the highly specialized skills of man's best friend.

Champion afghan hounds pose for the camera.

GOOD, BETTER, BEST

At dog shows, male and female dogs are judged separately, and prizes are awarded in many different categories. In the largest shows, judges may examine as many as 4,000 animals to select the best of each breed, the best of the seven major competitions, and finally, the best of the show.

MASTER CLASSES

In field trials, hunting dogs such as spaniels, pointers, and dachshunds are tested for their ability to follow scents, hunt game, and retrieve. The best of the younger dogs are awarded the title Junior Hunter, while the top mature dogs are called Master Hunters.

This border collie is competing in the high jump competition.

N THE SPOTLIGHT

From the very beginning, dogs have tarred in motion pictures and TV hows, stealing our hearts in the roles f Lassie, Rin Tin Tin, Benji, and Eddie, ist to name a few. On the set, he canine stars espond to hand ignals from their trainers, who remain just out of camera ange.

THEY'RE OFF!

At top speeds of 40 miles an hour, greyhounds are the fastest dogs on earth. Originally from the barren deserts of Africa and central Asia, the greyhound's speed was essential in catching prey.

GOOD DOG!

Dogs can win prizes purely for the way they behave. In obedience competitions, dogs of all types are judged to see how well they respond to commands.

The events include a broad jump, high jump, and retrieving.

Handlers ▶ exhibit their samoyeds for the judges.

▲ This poodle runs an agility course.

Sitting patiently while he gets groomed, this spaniel is getting ready for intense competition.

PUPPY LOVE

Sure they're cute and cuddly, but taking care of a puppy is no easy task. From birth to twelve weeks old, puppies must have constant supervision. Special care must go into their feeding, socialization, and training to assure a happy and healthy dog.

▲ LET'S EAT

Although unable to see or hear, one-day-old golden retriever pups already know where to find their mother's nipples for nursing.

▲ It's hard to believe this Siberian huskie puppy will one day weigh more than forty pounds.

◀ SLEEPYHEADS

For the first week of their lives, puppies will do nothing but eat and sleep. Up to the age of three months, puppies will go through periods of intense playfulness, exploration, and long sessions of deep sleep.

These puppies, only weeks old, huddle together for warmth when they sleep.

◀ THAT BITES!

Have you ever wondered why your puppy chews on slippers, clothing, and other household items? First, the puppy is simply playing. Second, the pup chews on hard objects to help its teeth grow in. And third, pups go through a pre-hunting stage and are practicing on whatever they can get their teeth on.

WOULD YOU ▶ LIKE TO PLAY?

Dog's have special body language to communicate to other dogs that their behavior is playful and not aggressive. When a dog's belly is close to the ground, and its rear end is raised, that means it's fun time.

▼ Bulldog puppies

▲ PLAY TIME

Playing is a vital part of puppyhood. These three German shorthair pointers are enjoying a game of tug of war. Such activities allow a growing pup to develop muscles, and teach it how to behave correctly with people and other dogs.

A DOG OF MY OWN

People who want to adopt a dog have many choices. Although purebred dogs make very good pets, mixed breeds are excellent companions as well. Many can be obtained free of charge. The important thing is to find the dog that is right for you.

SAVE THAT DOG!

Humane societies and other organizations run rescue and adoption programs for homeless dogs. Many of these groups can be found through local telephone listings, libraries, or the Internet—http://www.bulldog.org provides links to a number of rescue home pages.

PUPPY TALK

Though puppies may start to have human contact as young as three weeks old, they should stay with their mother for at least seven weeks. People choosing a puppy should avoid those who seem to be angry, overly timid, or sickly. These dogs are likely to develop problems as they get older.

Dalmatians are energetic dogs and need lots of space to exercise and play.

TEACHER'S PET

In order to live happily, dogs must be trained to behave properly. Experts say that every dog should learn to obey five basic commands: sit, down, stay, come, and drop it. Dogs should be praised when they respond properly. When they need to be corrected, a firm "No!" will do the job—there is nothing to be gained by yelling at a dog or hitting it.

▼ CHOW TIME

Like humans, dogs need to eat the right foods and drink plenty of water. The amount of food a dog needs depends on its age, size, and level of activity. Pregnant dogs also require special diets. Puppies have to eat three to four times a day, but full-grown dogs need only one or two daily meals.

▲ CHEW, CHEW, CHEW

Dogs love to gnaw on bones, but not all bones are healthy. Never give a dog bones that can splinter, such as turkey or pork bones—they can do serious damage if swallowed. Thick bones such as marrow bones are good, but they should be boiled first to kill any germs that might make the dog sick.

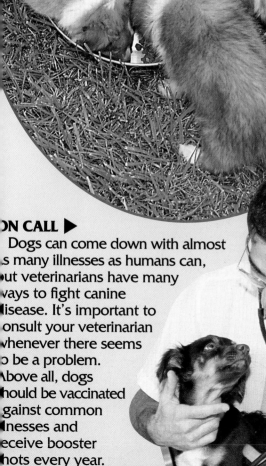

ON CALL ▶

Dogs can come down with almost as many illnesses as humans can, but veterinarians have many ways to fight canine disease. It's important to consult your veterinarian whenever there seems to be a problem. Above all, dogs should be vaccinated against common illnesses and receive booster shots every year.

▲ TAKING CARE

With proper care, a dog will live a long and healthy life. Dog owners need to groom their dogs regularly, making sure that the teeth, skin, and coat are in good condition. In general, dogs should be combed and brushed rather than bathed. Soap and water can strip natural oils from the skin and dry out the dog's coat.